Apples

Claire Llewellyn

SEA-TO-SEA

Mankato Collingwood London

This edition first published in 2005 by
Sea-to-Sea Publications
1980 Lookout Drive
North Mankato
Minnesota 56003

ISBN 1-932889-39-6

Printed in China

Library of Congress Control Number: 2004103744

2 4 6 8 9 7 5 3

Published by arrangement with the Watts Publishing Group Ltd, London

Designer: James Marks
Photography: Ray Moller unless otherwise credited
Acknowledgements: Nigel Cattlin/Holt Studios: 11, 13c, 13br. Copella Fruit Juices: 18. Peter Currell/
Ecoscene: 17. Pierre Gleizes/Still Pictures: 15. Willem Harinck/Holt Studios: 16. James Marks: 1,10b,
14. Sally Morgan/Ecoscene: 5br. Norman Rout/Ecoscene: 12b, 23t. Inga Spence/Holt Studios: 22b.
Thanks to our models: Freddy Marks, Casey Liu, Jakob Hawker, Reanne Birch

Contents

An apple is a fruit

Apples are a kind of fruit. They are sweet and crunchy to eat.

Apples can be red, green, or yellow.

▼ Most of us eat apples.

What kind of apples do you like best?

▼ Wasps eat apples, too. So do many other animals.

Apples are good for us

Apples are good for our bodies. Some people eat an apple every day to help them stay healthy.

▶ *Apples give us energy.*

Fruit is good for us.

What other fruits do you like to eat?

7

Looking at an apple

An apple has different parts.

▶ *On the outside of an apple are the stalk and the peel.*

Stalk

Peel

Inside are the flesh, the core, and the seeds.

Try planting apple seeds in potting soil. Keep the soil damp. In a few weeks, the seeds should start to grow.

Seeds

Flesh

Core

Apples grow on trees

Apples are the fruit of the apple tree.

▶ *This apple tree is growing in a backyard.*

These apple trees are growing on a farm.

Many fruit farms grow apples. The trees are planted in big fields called orchards.

Apple blossoms

In spring, apple trees
grow flowers called blossoms.

► *Blossoms
stay on the
apple tree
for two or
three weeks.*

Then tiny apples begin to grow on the tree.

In the blossoms is a yellow dust called pollen. For fruit to grow, pollen needs to move from one flower to another. Insects move the pollen as they feed.

The apples ripen

During the summer, the apples get bigger and bigger. By the fall, they are ripe.

▶ *Young apples are small and hard.*

Apples need plenty of sunshine and rain in order to grow.

▲ *Some apples change color as they get ripe.*

From orchard to store

Ripe apples are picked and put into boxes. Then they are taken to markets and stores.

▶ *The apples are picked by hand.*

We can buy many different kinds of apples in stores.

Apples have to be picked very carefully. What happens to an apple if you bump it or drop it?

Apple juice

Some apples are used to make apple juice. Machines crush the apples and press out the juice.

▶ *These apples are going into the apple press, where they will be made into juice.*

Apple juice is sold in bottles and cartons.

pure
apple
juice

pure
apple
juice

It takes two whole apples to make a glass of juice.

Cooking with apples

We often eat apples raw. We can also cook them in different ways.

What is your favorite apple treat?

Apples make delicious pies and desserts.

21

I know that...

1 Apples are a kind of fruit.

2 Apples are good for our bodies.

3 An apple has a stalk, peel, flesh, a core, and seeds.

4 Apples are the fruit of the apple tree.

5 Apple trees grow in orchards.

6 In spring, apple trees are covered in blossoms.

7 Apples grow in the summer. By fall, they are ripe.

8 Apples are picked when they are ripe. They are sold in stores and markets.

9 Apples are used to make apple juice.

10 We can cook apples in many different ways.

Index

About this book

I Know That! is designed to introduce children to the process of gathering information and using reference books, one of the key skills needed to begin more formal learning at school. For this reason, each book's structure reflects the information books children will use later in their learning career—with key information in the main text and additional facts and ideas in the captions. The panels give an opportunity for further activities, ideas, or discussions. The contents page and index are helpful reference guides.

The language is carefully chosen to be accessible to children just beginning to read. Illustrations support the text but also give information in their own right; active consideration and discussion of images is another key referencing skill. The main aim of the series is to build confidence—showing children how much they already know and giving them the ability to gather new information for themselves. With this in mind, the *I know that...* section at the end of the book is a simple way for children to revisit what they already know as well as what they have learned from reading the book.